Yellow Umbrella Books are published by Capstone Press
151 Good Counsel Drive, P.O. Box 669, Mankato, Minnesota 56002
http://www.capstone-press.com

Library of Congress Cataloging-in-Publication Data
Ring, Susan.
  Needs and wants / by Susan Ring.
    p. cm.
    Includes Index.
Summary: Presents the things that everyone needs, as well as things some people want, and invites the reader to consider his or her own wants and needs.
  ISBN 0-7368-2028-0 (hardcover : alk. paper)
  1. Motivation (Psychology) in children–Juvenile literature. 2. Need (Psychology)–Juvenile literature. 3. Desire–Juvenile literature. [1. Motivation (Psychology) 2. Need (Psychology). 3. Desire.] I. Title.
  BF723.M56R56 2003
  153.8–dc21

2003000930

Editorial Credits

Mary Lindeen, Editorial Director; Jennifer Van Voorst, Editor; Wanda Winch, Photo Researcher

Photo Credits

Cover: Creatas; Title Page: Stewart Cohen/Image Ideas, Inc.; Page 2: Galen Rowell/Corbis; Page Neil Beer/PhotoDisc; Page 4: Ryan McVay/PhotoDisc; Page 5: Rubber Ball Productions; Page 6: Rob Van Petten/DigitalVision; Page 7: Bob Winsett/Image Ideas, Inc.; Page 8: John Connell/Corbis; Page 9: Comstock; Page 10: Comstock; Page 11: Image Source/elektraVision; Page 12: Ellen Skye/Index Stock; Page 13: Stewart Cohen/Image Ideas, Inc.; Page 14: SWP, Incorporated/Brand X Pictures; Page 15: Rob Van Petten/DigitalVision; Page 16: Doug Menuez/PhotoDisc

1 2 3 4 5 6 08 07 06 05 04 03

Needs and Wants

by Susan Ring

Consultant: Dwight Herold, Ed.D., Past President,
Iowa Council for the Social Studies

Yellow Umbrella Books

an imprint of Capstone Press
Mankato, Minnesota

There are things we all need.

They help us live.

We need homes.

Homes give us shelter.

We need clothes.

Clothes keep us warm.

We need food.

Food keeps us healthy.

There are also things we want. But we do not always need them.

We may want ice cream.
But we do not need it to live.

We may want a ball.
But we do not need it to live.

We may want a bike.
But we do not need it to live.

We have to have the things we need.

We choose to have the things we want.

What do you need?
What do you want?

Words to Know/Index

Word Count: 107
Early-Intervention Level: 7